Behind the Scenes!!

07

STORY AND ART BY BISCO HATORI

Behind the Scenes!!

07

CONTENTS

Special Thanks!!

Nakajima-sama
Okazaki-sama
Everyone on the editorial staff
Everyone involved in publishing this book

Forêt-sama
guse ars-sama
Misaki Kamata-sama
Ueki-sama
Shinya Hokimoto-sama
Kana (NIZAKANA)-sama
Tanisima-sama
Everyone who helped with research and ideas during the series

The Staff

★Super Helpers!★
Haruka Chino-sama
Madoka Shida-sama
Pochi Takahashi-sama
Terashima-sama

And everyone who read this book!!

Thank you very much!!

Bisco.H
2018. sep.

She's got great sense, so she's the boss lady of style!! Plus, she makes sweets!!

She looks cute, and her nickname is...

Secret Boss Lady

六夏 Rocca / 梅子 Umeko

Congrats on completing the series!♡ ↑

Also an awesome fortune-teller!!

The indomitable pro assistant!! With gobs of experience!

おいしいもの
大好き仲間♥

並木 美樹
Miki Namiki

↓ For some reason, I liked this guy!♡

Good job on Behind the Scenes!!

I tell fortunes on the sly! Twitter: @nmiki1101 ↓

Working together was so much fun! ↑

Behind the Scenes of Behind the Scenes!! 3

A natural queen when it comes to love of animals and sports!! With a deep appreciation of orangutans!

And a sudden interest in penguins!

Shii Tsunokawa
角川しい

LEND ME YOUR STRENGTH, RANMARU!
YOU GOT IT...
...DIRECTOR!
THE DAYS PASS...
...AND I CONTINUE TO EVOLVE!
BEHIND THE SCENES!! VOLUME 7 – THE END

"I NEED TO THINK MORE."
DESPITE WHAT HE SAID.
I'm off to travel the world!
It was a sudden decision!
S-seriously?!
Wherever he goes, he works part-time jobs and sells art.
Sometimes he comes back.
Hi, Ryuji! Can I spend the night?
Street at night
GACK
THAT'S JUST THE WAY HE IS...
...BUT HE KNOWS WHERE HOME IS.
SO?
DID YOU READ THE SCRIPT?
Y... YES.
AM I GOOD ENOUGH TO WORK ON IT?
DON'T BE SILLY!
AS FOR US...
Film Art Association
Ryuji Goda
Their Hands
BFF
GOT IT?
THIS TIME, I'M AIMING FOR A BIGGER PRIZE!

APPARENTLY, TOMU WAS IN IT TOO.
DID YOU NOTICE?
WAS HE A ZOMBIE THAT GOT BLOWN AWAY AT THE AIRPORT?
OR MAYBE A ZOMBIE THE GANGSTERS KILLED?
OR ONE THAT FELL FROM THE ROOF?
AND TOMU...
...WENT TO AMERICA WITH MAASA!!
BUT THE NATURE OF THEIR RELATIONSHIP IS STILL UNCLEAR.
Hollywood?! Take me! Take me!
Why you?!
Are they living together?
I don't know.
IS THAT FROM IZUMI?
I GOT ONE TOO.
HE'S STILL WANDERING AROUND.

SHE'S GOT MORNING SICKNESS.
glup glup
What?!
YOU'RE HAVING ANOTHER ONE?!
KLATTER
Oops, sorry.
Ugh Ugh
You never change...
HOW ARE THINGS WITH SOH?
You gonna make it official?
I...I NEED TO FOCUS ON MY WORK FIRST!
ARE YOU KIDDING?
I SAW YOUR PROMO VIDEO.
EVERYONE'S CLAMORING FOR YOU NOW!
ARTWORK BY
DID YOU SEE THE MOVIE?
KING OF THE ZOMBIES 2!
YEAH!! MAASA'S NAME WAS IN THE CREDITS!!
AFTER GRADUATION...
...I JOINED A VISUAL-ARTS PRODUCTION COMPANY.
MAASA HAS BEEN STUDYING IN AMERICA FOR TWO YEARS...
...THROUGH THE GRACES OF THE ARTIST SHE MET THAT DAY.
King of

ka
chak
OH...
RAN-MARU, YOU CAME!
IT'S BEEN A WHILE!
Six years later...
NICE PLACE!
IT'S SMALL...
...SO I RENT STUDIO SPACE TOO.
glance
WHERE'S RUKA?
Uh...
SHE'S NOT JOINING US TODAY.

ding dong
403

YES...
...NOW I CAN PROUDLY SAY THAT...
...THIS IS WHERE I BELONG.
YOU'LL BE THE NEW CHIEF STARTING IN APRIL.
You belong here, right?
Huh?!
Cleaning before graduation
Good luck, Ranmaru!
You'll negotiate the budget and recruit new members and...
Huuh?!

YES, I DID GET A TRANSMISSION.
THIS IS YET ANOTHER MOMENT...
...LEADING TO THE FUTURE.
I SAID I WAS GOING TO TRAVEL AFTER GRADUATION...
...BUT FIRST I NEED TO THINK MORE.
YEAH, THAT'S RIGHT!!
I'M GONNA MAKE MY SUPERHERO SHOW DEBUT!!
In a minor role
OF COURSE I ACCEPTED!
A GOD OF HORROR INVITED ME!
Business card
I'M GOING TO STRIVE LIKE MY LIFE DEPENDS ON IT!

MY DAD CALLED THE OTHER DAY, AND I...
...TOLD HIM ABOUT THE FILM.
"YOU'VE FINALLY RETURNED TO YOUR PATH."
THAT'S WHAT HE SAID.
HE KNEW THIS WAS GONNA HAPPEN!
That Baldy!
THAT'S A DAD FOR YOU!
Tee hee
WHY ARE YOU FILMING THIS?
Tee hee!
I WANT TO TREASURE THIS MOMENT.
HMM...
HAVE YOU...
...RECEIVED ANY TRANSMISSIONS LATELY?
HUH?
YOU KNOW, THOSE ORDERS YOU GET...
...FROM OUTER SPACE.

I feel better after changing!
RAN-MARU...
...THANKS FOR BEING THE SUB'S SUB!
REC 00:07:31
I FILMED THE ART SQUAD FOR PRACTICE...
...AND SAW HOW HARD THEY WORK.
AND FILMING THAT...
...INSPIRED THIS FILM.
Ryuji Goda (22)
Economics, Year 4

Thanks, Soh!
OH!
THERE'S IZUMI!
STANDING-BY?
ABOUT WHAT YOU WERE SAYING...
SOH...
...YOU WERE TOTALLY RIGHT!
RAN HAS ALWAYS BEEN THERE FOR ME!
BUT IS IT STRANGE TO LIKE YOUR COUSIN?
Soh!
YES?

klatta klatta
WHOOO
IF I HADN'T BEEN THERE ...

Unbelievable!
YES...
...THAT'S HOW EVENTS UNFOLD.
IF WE HADN'T CHANGED LOCA-TIONS...
...AND IF WE HADN'T FILMED IN IZUMI'S NEIGHBOR-HOOD...
...AND IF TOMU HADN'T DROPPED THE ARM...
MAKE ARTIST
SENHASU JO
WEB
MAIL
AND IF ON THAT DAY...
...AT THAT MOMENT...

YOU...
...HAVEN'T CHANGED AT ALL!!
HUH?
Ha ha ha
YOU ALWAYS DID STUFF LIKE THAT...
...IN ELE-MENTARY SCHOOL TOO!
SERI-OUSLY?
SO YOU'VE...
...ALWAYS BEEN THIS WAY?!
It's not from amnesia?
Pat ★
TRY AS YOU MIGHT...
How his accident happened (probably)
...YOU'RE STILL SPACEY!

GAH!
SP
SHH
UWAAH
IZUMI?!
BLUUH
...
H-HOW DID THAT HAPPEN...
...AFTER YOU MENTIONED THE SPOUTS?!
SA-MURA...

tik
I HOPE THEY FOUND THE ARM.
IT'S ALMOST TIME FOR THE FOUNTAINS TO GO OFF.
BE CAREFUL. THERE ARE SPOUTS OVER THERE.
Lemme see!
WHAT A RARE COLOR!
stagger
HUH?
IZUMI?
tok
TIK

NO!
THAT'S MY ARM! I DROPPED IT!
What?!
IT'S MINE!
I PUT MY HEART AND SOUL INTO IT!
HMM...
...THIS ARM...
...IS WELL-MADE.
DID YOU MAKE THIS?
RAN-MARU...
...I NEED A POTTY BREAK.
fwuf fwuf
You're on standby!
OKAY!
Hm? Where's Soh?
She went on an errand!

RAN-MARU! LET'S GO!
RANMA-RU!
...IS A PLACE ...
...FOR ME!
chatter chatter
Ugh...
N...

KLAKK
their hands
29 — 1
ANYONE WOULD PRESERVE THIS MOMENT...
...IN THEIR PHOTO ALBUM OF MEMORIES.
AND WITHIN THAT VIBRANT PICTURE...

HEY, KURISU!
What should I do with this?
RAN-MARU!
Do me a favor!
RAN!
WHAT AN ODD FEEL-ING...
WHY...
...AM I HERE?
All ready!
Camera's rolling!
SCENE 29! TAKE 1!
READY AND ...

SOMEONE THERE FROM THE START.
UM ...
IZU M-I-I
I HAVE TO GO. TELL ME MORE LATER!
Sorry!
Soh! Will you run to the convenience store?
Okay!
RAN-MARU!
IS THE GORE READY?
YEP!
RANMARU! DOES THIS LOOK RIGHT?
YEP! LOOKS GOOD!

hup
WHY ARE YOU WATCHING RAN-MARU?
?!!
BOO
THAT VOICE... IS THAT YOU, IZUMI?
I'M SUBBING FOR TOMU!
Yeah!
I'M IN THE NIGHTMARE SCENE.
SO YOU LIKE RAN-MARU, HUH?
YOU WOULD MAKE A GOOD COUPLE.
N-NO!
smile smile
NO? YOU HARDLY TAKE YOUR EYES OFF HIM.
B-BUT I...
I keep switching love interests!!
AH
WA
S-SOH?!
Until recently, I was hung up on you!
DON'T BE HARD ON YOURSELF.
SOMEDAY YOU'LL AWAKEN TO SOMEONE CLOSER TO YOUR HEART...
...THAN ANYONE ELSE.

Tomu!! Why're you just standing here?!
chatter
...
chatter
HUH?
YIKES!
A HUMAN ARM!
yiiiikes
KYAAAAH
CALL THE POLICE!!
WAAAAAAH
A murder?!
It's gotta be!!
PANIC
WHAT A DISASTER! ☆
FORTY-FIVE DEGREES!
ALL RIGHT!
NOW MAKE IT STABLE!

MAYBE IT DROPPED ALONG THE WAY.
Hmmm...
I HOPE IT ISN'T ANYWHERE CONSPICUOUS...
HUH?
LOOK AT ALL THOSE FOUNTAIN SPOUTS...
Straight from the ground
No way!
I used powder clay for the bones!
They'll melt in water!
BUT THEY ONLY ERUPT AT CERTAIN TIMES, RIGHT?
YES. AT 1:00 AND 3:00 P.M.
!!!
I'm going after Tomu!!!
I can't trust him alone!
ME EITHER!
IZUMI! I NEED YOU HERE!
HUH?
WE'RE SHORT ON TIME.
SORRY FOR THE SUDDEN REQUEST, BUT...
HUH?
Me?
Huff

WE WERE FILMING AROUND THE PARK WHEN...
WHAT?
AN ARM IS MISSING!!
DOES ANYONE KNOW WHERE IT IS?!
IT'S IN A BLACK BAG!
DIDN'T YOU BRING IT, TOMU?
HUH?
OH NO!!!
I dunno!!!
I'll go look
YOU dim-WIT!!!

About *Behind the Scenes!!*

What serialization taught me...

Stories about professions are hard!

It's about amatuers, but still...

But character and story won't come together!
What? I've got a great topic!

A whole mountain of stuff didn't work right...

Above all, however, it was fun!

I met a lot of behind-the-scenes creators who showed me how fathomless their world is, and each day I was inspired and impressed by their incredible skills and enthusiasm.

Thank you so much!

Yo, Riichiro!
Um, aren't you and Goda...
...dating now?
Apparently, only I think so.
Heh heh heh
We haven't even held hands!!
Why is that?!
He's just busy with the film!
REC 00:05:36
Y... yes.
It happened at about 2:30.
Maasa was the first to notice.
Soh Kobora (18)
Kokuto School for Girls
Literature, Year 1

...BECAUSE I WANTED MY OLD SELF TO DISAPPEAR.
HEH ...
Whew...
Isn't chance amazing?
ANYWAY...
...IT'S FUNNY HOW THINGS TURNED OUT.
HM? SOH?
SHE'S LIKE A SISTER TO ME! REALLY!
BESIDES, SOH IS...
Heh...
OOH!
ISN'T THAT SWEET?
...They're both so attractive! ♡
DON'T THEY LOOK GOOD TOGETHER?
Geh!
HOW CAN THEY CUDDLE IN PUBLIC?!
Now I'm even more scared!
Pout

HEY! THERE'S IZUMI SAMURA!
Are they filming? Let's go see!
SHH! NOT SO LOUD!
Yeah!
HE DOESN'T REMEM-BER US...
...SO HE MIGHT FEEL BAD.
UM, WERE WE...
...IN ELEMEN-TARY SCHOOL TOGETH-ER?
WE GO WAY BACK!
I don't remember you, but still!
Feel free to watch!
Yeah! Fifth grade! I'm Ueda!!
Yeah, I wanna watch!
I'm Shimo-mura!!
Phew
REC 00:12:08
YES...
...I'M MORE FIRMLY GROUNDED NOW.
I USED TO WONDER ABOUT MY ACCIDENT...
...BE-CAUSE I WAS SCARED.
MAYBE I CAN'T REMEMBER THE PAST...

I'LL BE A HERO STUNTMAN...
...AND YOU'LL MAKE THE VILLAINS!
We'll work together! In Hollywood!!
BY THE TIME YOU MAKE IT THAT FAR, I PLAN TO BE A RICH WIFE WITH CHILDREN!
BECAUSE I FINALLY REALIZED SOMETHING.
IF I KEEP DOING THIS, I'LL BE SINGLE FOREVER!!
I've missed three singles parties for this!
Can't pursue two goals at once
Ah ha ha ha
Hmm~
...
IN THAT CASE, MAYBE I COULD—
HM?
THE GOD OF MODELING!!
HE'S HAVING AN EXHIBIT?!
And nearby!!
HE HAS A STUDIO AROUND HERE!
SERIOUSLY?!
THAT ARTIST...
Special Modeling
The Cutting Edge of Fantasy
OUR NEW LOCATION IS GREAT!!
YEAH!
IT'S SPACIOUS AND SCENIC!
FOUNTAINS TURN ON...
...AT SET TIMES THROUGHOUT THE DAY.
And getting permission was easy.
SAMURA?

NO, THE GENIUS IS...
IT'S LIKE A DREAM!
So pretty!
WOW!
Huh?
YOU MADE ALL THAT FROM PLASTIC BOTTLES?!
THEY'RE EVEN BETTER THAN EX-PECTED.
Thanks!
THE L.E.D. LIGHTS ARE A GOOD TOUCH!
TH-THANKS!
CREATING A "BEAUTIFUL NIGHTMARE" WAS AN INTEREST-ING TASK!
I WAS WORRIED AT FIRST...
...BUT THEN THE IDEAS FLOODED IN!
blush
YOU'RE A TOTAL SHOW-OFF!
But you fake modesty.
MAASA! I HAVE AN IDEA!!

I MADE THESE OF COURSE!!
PTUMP
Actors
WHOA... THEY LOOK REAL!
THEY'RE GROSS!
COOL!!
YOU KILLED IT, MAASA!!
Tee hee hee
I PUT EXTRA EFFORT INTO REALISTIC TEXTURE AND WEIGHT!!
IN THE END, THE BODY PARTS TURN OUT TO BE FAKE...
Izumi's neighborhood
(Two hours by car)
...BUT THE PRO-TAGONISTS DON'T KNOW THAT...
...SO THEY HAD TO SEEM REAL!
BUT MY SKILLS FELL SHORT...
POKE
They feel fake to the touch!
NUH-UH! YOU'RE A GENIUS!!

IN THIS SCENE, THE PROTAGONISTS FACE THEIR CHILDHOOD SINS...
...SO THIS'LL REPRESENT THEIR PSYCHOLOGICAL STATE!!
02:19
GODA WAS AWESOME!
LIKE, SUPER RESOURCEFUL!
AND EVERYONE GOT TOTALLY INTO IT!!
Humanities and Sciences, Year 2
Tomu Tenba (20)
REC 00:03:06
Maasa Rokubu (21)
Marketing, Year 3
WE HAD TO MAKE OUR OWN LUCK.
AND DECIDING TO FILM IN IZUMI'S NEIGHBORHOOD PROVED TO BE A FATEFUL DECISION.
HM? WHAT WAS I IN CHARGE OF?

how Weather
Chance of Rain
0%
Have a nice day! ♡
ZSSH
The weather turned traitor!
...
HEY, SEAWEED HEAD!
NOW WHAT?! WHAT A PAIN! I CLEARED MY SCHEDULE FOR THIS!
RIN... I THOUGHT YOU'D CHANGED!
WELL, YOU'RE NOT PAYING ME!
AND I'M EXPENSIVE!
Spoiled actor
chatter
UH-OH. WE DON'T HAVE A BACKUP LOCATION.
I CAN'T PUSH ANY HARDER...
AND I HAVE OTHER PLANS!
GRIN
INTERESTING...
I'LL FILM IN THE RAIN!
BUT IT WON'T MATCH THE PREVIOUS FOOTAGE!
NAH, IT'LL BE BETTER THIS WAY!
ZSSH

DOOM
What the?!
No filming in the park!! That means you, Shichikoku University students! We'll call the police!
Absolutely not!
What's going on here?!
HANEIKE'S GROUP DAMAGED PARK PROPERTY WHILE FILMING HERE YESTERDAY.
Give me morrre!
KRAKK
THAT JERK! WAS IT ON PURPOSE?!
No! Sorry!
WHY?! I RESERVED IT A WEEK AGO!
HELLO? UH-HUH... I SEE.
IS THERE ANYWHERE ELSE SIMILAR?!
NO. NOT AROUND HERE.
Gyaah Gyaah
And then later...
I'LL FIND A NEW LOCATION, SO STAY ANOTHER YEAR!
Teasing
Shut up!

WE CAME TO WATCH! ☆
Don't mind us! ☆
GODA'S DIRECTORIAL COMEBACK IS SURE TO BE INSTRUCTIVE!
YAY, UICHIRO! ♡♡
CAN YOU DO ALL THIS AND STILL GRAD-UATE?
Tee hee hee!
QUIET! I'LL WRITE MY THESIS LATER!
WELL, DON'T WORK TOO HARD! ☆
TAKE ALL THE TIME YOU NEED...
...BE-CAUSE WE'LL BE AROUND TO HELP! ♡
Already slated for a fifth year
The Super Seniors
THAT'S RIGHT, GODA.
OR I'LL WITH-HOLD MY AP-PROVAL.
YOU GUYS...
GET LOST, YOU RIFFRAFF!!!
Whoa! What a grumpy director!
Yikes! ☆
This doesn't bode well...
YOU'RE MAKIN' A MOVIE!
CAN I BE IN IT?!
Put me in!
chatter
THEN CRE-ATE A NEW ROLE!!
NO, THE CAST IS SET!
chatter
WANNA USE MY ACTION FIGURES?
You can borrow 'em!
chatter
WE'LL HELP WITH SFX!
I C-CAME TO HELP.
Oh, thanks!
chatter
You'll use a student from another school but not us?!

LIKE WHEN THE CREW FIRST ASSEMBLED ...
I'M FURI, PRODUCTION ASSISTANT.
I'M AOKI, CAMERAMAN.
I'M AKAI, ASSISTANT PHOTOGRAPHER AND LIGHTING.
I'M HIDA...
...THE ASSISTANT DIRECTOR.
I'M SURPRISED UICHIRO ACCEPTED.
I'm Kurokawa on lighting!
I'm Tomu! I carry stuff and ♡ wear animal costumes!
HE'S PROBABLY THE HAPPIEST ABOUT THE CHIEF'S COMEBACK!
MAYBE!!
Hee hee!
I ALREADY HAVE A FULL CREW ...
...so why the big crowd?!
TA
DUM

...SOMETIMES IT'S COMICAL...
...OR HALLUCINATORY OR LIKE A MUSICAL.
IT'S SCARY BUT BEAUTIFUL...
...MAKING VIEWERS LAUGH AND CRY.
REC 00:02:43
IT PORTRAYS THE HUMAN SPIRIT.
Izumi Samura (23)
Economics, Year 4
HOW VERY LIKE RYUJI!
REC 00
SO MUCH HAPPENED...
...DURING FILMING.
Ruka Enjoji (22)
Economics, Year 4
AND THERE WERE EARLY SIGNS OF TROUBLE.

IT'S HIS GIRLFRIEND'S.
HIS FRIENDS RECEIVE BOXES TOO...
...BUT THEY'RE ALL AFRAID TO TELL EACH OTHER.
EMOTIONS SURFACE AS THEY FEEL EACH OTHER OUT.
Suspicion
Jealousy
Vanity
Repentance
YOU'D THINK IT WOULD BE DARK, BUT...

REC 00:00:24
AT FIRST, I WAS SURPRISED.
I THOUGHT HE WOULD WRITE...
...A DRAMA ABOUT YOUTH OR FAMILY.
Ranmaru Kurisu (20)
Humanities and Sciences, Year 2
BUT HORROR?
ONE DAY, A UNIVERSITY STUDENT...
...RECEIVES AN ARM IN THE MAIL.
NO WAY...

...GODA FINISHED HIS SCRIPT.
their hands

LATER, RUKA RUSHED TO THE PLAY-HOUSE...
...AND WAS POSITIVELY RADIANT.
Sorry, every-one!!
Oh! You're already working on them!
All right!
Let's finish you up!!
YAAY
clap clap
clap clap clap
AND...
...AROUND THE TIME THAT THE SCHOOL FESTIVAL CAME TO AN END...
Now Ruka won't Quit!
Hurray!

A few words on portraying specialized fields in *Behind the Scenes!!*

Should any exaggerations in presentation or mistakes due to my poor understanding arise in the course of applying my research to the manga, the responsibility is entirely mine. Thank you for your understanding.

Behind the Scenes of Behind the Scenes!! 2

↑Behind the Scenes!!
Good work on the series! ♥♥

She's a master artist who always does the unexpected. And she admires a conch-shell player!

Good luck!!

Shizuru Onda
恩多志弦

Doodle Artisans #1&2

When there's an opening, she provides god-quality doodles in copious amounts!

LOL

Her *Saint Seiya* Saga T-shirt collection※ is legendary.

※ Her collection of T-shirt designs featuring Saga

Keiko Misaki
岬景子

LAST
SCENE

MY COURAGE TODAY...
...WILL CARRY ME INTO THE FUTURE.

HOW DARE YOU?!
SHUMP
HA HA!
I REALLY TOLD HIM OFF!
I WILL NEVER...
...FORGET THIS DAY.

"WHAT DO YOU REALLY WANT TO DO?!"
TAKE RESPON-SIBILITY ...
...AND EVOLVE!!
URGH ...

I KNOW WHY A STRONG GUY LIKE YOU...
...UNDER-STANDS A GUY LIKE ME.
THE TRUTH IS...
...THAT FROM THE DEEP SEA INSIDE EVERY-ONE...
YOU NEED TO STRIVE.
YOU NEED TO DO...
...WHAT YOU ACTUALLY WANT TO DO!
IF YOU DON'T WANT HER TO QUIT, THEN SAY SO!
"STRIVE!
IF YOU WANT HER TO STAY WITH YOU, THEN SAY SO!
TRY TO EVOLVE!"

...LIKE A SARDINE WITH ITS GLITTERY SCALES ...
WATCHING IN SILENCE CAN BE HELPFUL...
...BUT SOMETIMES PEOPLE NEED TO HEAR CERTAIN WORDS.
HUH?
BUT YOU'RE TOO SCARED.
YOU'RE AFRAID ...
...SHE MIGHT REJECT YOU.
JUST LIKE WITH YOUR MOVIE ...
...YOU ALWAYS RUN FROM WHAT'S IMPOR-TANT.
"WHAT IF MY TALENT HAS DRIED UP?!"
WHAT ARE YOU—
BUT ...
...NOW I GET IT.

"SARDINES ARE WEAK...
...BUT THEY'RE ALSO BRAVE."
ka chak...
WHO IS IT?
RAN-MARU?
GODA...
...GO MEET RUKA WHEN SHE GETS HERE.
IF I CAN HELP EVEN A LITTLE...

...SHE MAY DO AS SHE PLEASES WITH HER FUTURE!!
"RANMARU..."
"...SARDINES SCATTER THEIR SCALES LIKE GLITTER...
...TO SAVE OTHER SARDINES FROM DANGER."

YOTA ...
THIS IS RIDICULOUS!
YOU'RE COMING WITH ME, RUKA!
I'LL WHIP YOU INTO SHAPE!
HUH ?!
EX-CUSE ME!
BUT I AM RUKA'S MOTHER!
I KNOW HOW HARD SHE WORKS ...
...BUT I NEVER HAD THE COURAGE TO SPEAK UP.
WHAT ?!
AS HER MOTHER ...
...I SAY...

...THERE ARE PEOPLE AROUND WHO CAN HELP.
RUKA?
JUST GO.
I'LL HANDLE THIS.
YOTA?
I'VE BEEN THINKING.
I'M GOING TO WORK HARD TO SUPPORT THE FAMILY...
...SO YOU CAN FOLLOW YOUR HEART.
YOU NEVER UNDER-STAND THAT.
HUH?
PEOPLE CALLED ME ILLEGITI-MATE...
...SO WHEN WE FIRST MET...
"YOTA?"
"I'M RUKA.
I'M YOUR SISTER NOW!"
THAT...
...MEANT A LOT TO ME.

WE'LL MANAGE BY OUR-SELVES...
...UNTIL RUKA GETS HERE!!
BUT ...
RUKA ...
... HASN'T REAL-IZED IT...
...BUT SHE'S LIKE ME.
SHE LOSES HOPE TOO EASILY.
SHE GIVES UP...
...ON HERSELF AND OTHERS.
BUT THE TRUTH IS...

FROM NOW ON, I'LL RAISE RUKA!
YOTA ?!
HE HUNG UP!
WHERE THE HECK'S THE CHIEF?!
IN THE CLUB ROOM.
YOU WANT I SHOULD KIDNAP HER?!
What're we gonna do?!
Does my costume go like this?
I can't do my eye makeup!
NO.
MAASA... SOH...
YOU CAN DO THEIR FOUNDATION AND WIGS, RIGHT?
Y-YEAH. RUKA SHOWED US.
GOOD.

RUKA'S AUNT FOUND OUT?!
I CHECKED THE SECURITY CAMERA!
AND THEY WERE YOUR FRIENDS!
THEY MADE A FOOL OF ME!
THEY ...
THEY DID THIS FOR ME.
I HELPED THEM.
RUKA DIDN'T DO ANY-THING.
SO LET HER GO TO THE—
NO, I WON'T ALLOW IT!
SHE NEEDS TO LEARN SOME RULES!
THAT WOMAN IS THE ONE WHO NEEDS TO LEAVE!
!!

Welcome to the 58th Shichikoku University Festival!
Tacos
Delicious! Tako-yaki
Let the festivities begin!!
Shichi-koku Festival
Theater Troupe Ptoleminius
Blue Night
12:00~
16:00~
DOOR CONCERT
HUH?
RUKA ISN'T HERE YET?!
BUT WE NEED TO GET INTO MAKEUP!!
Yota Kurisu
080-
BVVVT
HELLO? YOTA?
WHAT?!

"ACCORDING TO RUMOR, IT WAS GODA WHO TOLD EVERYONE SHE'S QUITTING!"
WHO ELSE...
...COULD HAVE GIVEN HER THIS?
IT WAS...
Let's have a lavish send-off!
I brought all my savings!
...A PRICELESS GIFT...
...FROM A CLUMSY PERSON.

...THAT I'VE SPENT DAY AND NIGHT DEDICATING MYSELF...
...TO MY CRAFT!
I CAN'T STOP ...
...BECAUSE I'M SO FULL OF STRENGTH ...
...AND I'M SO HAPPY!
...
"GUESS HOW SHE GOT SO MUCH WORK!"

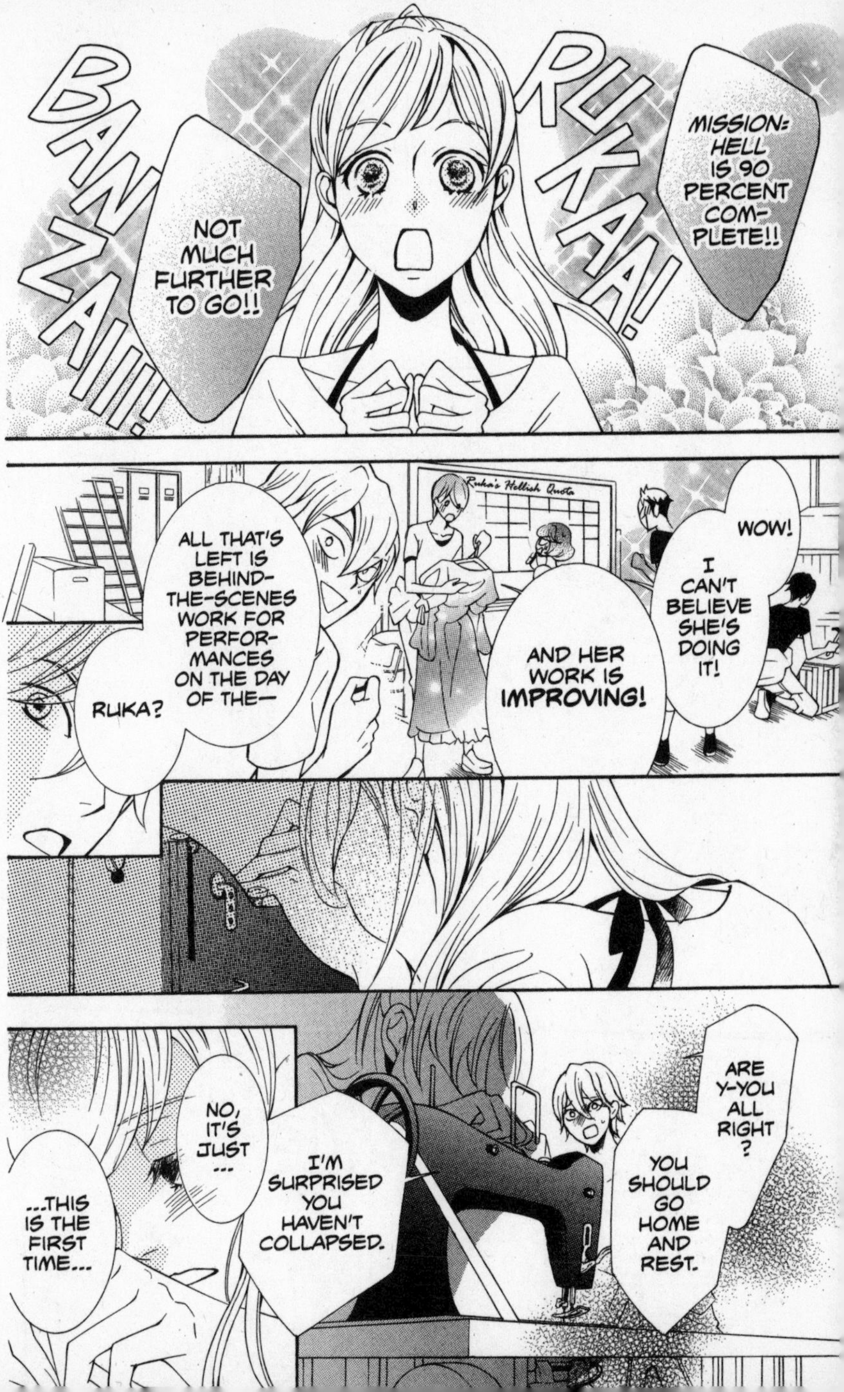
RUKAAI!
MISSION: HELL IS 90 PERCENT COM-PLETE!!
NOT MUCH FURTHER TO GO!!
BANZAIIII!!
Ruka's Hellish Quota
WOW!
I CAN'T BELIEVE SHE'S DOING IT!
AND HER WORK IS IMPROVING!
ALL THAT'S LEFT IS BEHIND-THE-SCENES WORK FOR PERFOR-MANCES ON THE DAY OF THE—
RUKA?
ARE Y-YOU ALL RIGHT?
YOU SHOULD GO HOME AND REST.
I'M SURPRISED YOU HAVEN'T COLLAPSED.
NO, IT'S JUST...
...THIS IS THE FIRST TIME...

Doin' Research Part ④
Kamata mainly does hairstyling.
She's stunning!
I thoroughly research the original characters!
And I discuss them with the actors!
I try to grasp the characters even better than they do! ☆
This must make the authors happy!
It's hard work!
But when I hear the audience's applause...
...I can't wait to do more!
Which means the applause even reaches backstage...
There you have it, theater lovers!

Ranmaru isn't coming home this year.
But I want to tease him!
He's such a brat!
The Kurisu family
Cut!! That's a wrap! Good work!!
It's a wrap!!
Thanks, Ruka!!
SKWIK
Art meeting
Wigs
A B C D E F G H I
Filming 1-2
Poster Photography
Filming
GOOD!
Costumes
A B C
Filming On location!

KYAH! A SEA-FOOD GIFT SET! ♡
Abalone and sea snails!
oiled sardines
Salted Squid
And there's a letter ...
Good luck, my sardine boy!! Dad
Sardines!
Again
Sardines!
Sardines!
Yay!
WHY SAR-DINES?
BECAUSE THEY'RE A WEAK FISH.
ON LAND, THEY DIE RIGHT AWAY.
Ohhh...
Sardines...
...are wimps.
SO EVER SINCE I WAS A KID...
"...LET'S TALK ABOUT SAR-DINES..."
"RAN-MARU ..."
...

I CAME TO HELP.
Kyah! Soh! Thanks!
This is how to put on a wig!
Okay!
...THE MORE I SEE THAT EVERYONE...
...IS FRAGILE AND CLUMSY...
Oh! Tattoo stickers?
Yeah! I designed them on the computer!
Tomu! That goes on the right!
...AND TRYING THEIR HARDEST.
Gah
Oh, right! I need to reverse the image!
That was close!
※When printing tattoo stickers, reverse the image.
RAN-MARU!!
YOU GOT A PACKAGE FROM HOME!!

I THOUGHT YOU DIDN'T LIKE THAT THING!
Ah ha ha
ACTUALLY, IT'S PRETTY HELP-FUL!
"NO WAY! IT'S SO UNFASHION-ABLE!"
"WHAT?!"
gwup
IF I'M GONNA DO THIS, I CAN'T WORRY ABOUT APPEAR-ANCES!
Go girl!!
hustle
We've got work too!
THE WORLD...
...GLITTERS IN THE DISTANCE...
...BUT THE CLOSER I GET...

I have renewed vigor!!
YEP !!
FOR REASONS UNKNOWN !!
I'M GONNA WORK MY TAIL OFF! AT HOME TOO!!
OH ...
THAT'S GOOD.
SO SHE DOESN'T NEED THIS EXTRA KEY I CUT FOR YOU?
Tom's dad.
GODA SAID YOU NEEDED 24/7 ACCESS, SO—
MMPH
GWOOSH
I don't mind!
But I'm Glad it worked out!
Really? A Ghost?
How odd!
RUKA, YOU'VE GOT A MEETING!
BUT, UM...
Umph!
Handy Hauler
Kinjiro
by Goda

OH WELL.
THERE'S ...
...ONLY ONE MONTH UNTIL THE FESTIVAL!
August
Hida—makeup/prop meeting
Hida—redesign
13° Haneike—Costume
15° Dance Club Meeting
16° Virtual Passage Meeting
Dance/Design UP1
Riichi—Deliver costumes
17°Ptoleminus Meeting
Fabric/prop shopping
Ptoleminus costume meeting
Costume
Hida—costume
Tenba Motors
HUH?
YOUR AUNT PROBLEM IS SOLVED?
thumbs up

AT DAWN! AND IN A RUSH!
This place is haunted!
I'll never come again!
Hmph!
OH...
I was working so hard I didn't notice.
Sigh
YOU LOOK... A BIT FRAZZLED.
Tee hee...
FRAZZZZ
OH NO!!
I can't show myself to you like this!
HERE. I'LL FIX IT.
YOU'RE SO SKILLED...
IT'S MY ONLY MERIT...
...BUT...
...I WON'T BE AROUND TO DO THIS MUCH LONGER.
Ha ha ha!
Gah!
I have to go!

CREAK
WOO...
...OOOO... ...OOO!
tweet tweet
HUH?
SHE LEFT?
YES...

Aunt
Ruka
Yota
Current location
Gasp
SLAMM
IT'S NEXT TO...
... AUNT'S!
Is that okay?
mutter grumble
This is an outrage!
I CAN USE ...
...THE SEWING MACHINE IN THIS ROOM !!
Kyaah! I can work! Kyaah!
ZZZ
silence
"GOT IT, YOTA?
AFTER SHE FALLS ASLEEP, PRESS THIS BUTTON."
CREAK

BOOM BOOM
THRUM
IT'S DANGEROUS, SO YA GOTTA VACATE DA PREMISES! ☆
VREEN
Guard
?!
I WAS STUCK IN THE LIVING ROOM FOR THREE HOURS!!
They just now left!!
HUH?
WELL, IF YOTA WANTS TO CHANGE THE HOUSE...
Or whatever...
CHANGE THE HOUSE?
HE ISN'T EVEN YOUR REAL BROTHER!
AUNT!!
Pat
RUKA...
...CAN WE SWITCH ROOMS TONIGHT?
HM?
SHUV
THE SUN SHINES THROUGH MY WINDOWS TOO EARLY...
...AND I NEED TO STUDY LATE TONIGHT.
SHUV
HUH?!
WHAT?!
WAIT! I'M NOT DONE TALKING!
I D-DON'T MIND...
...BUT MY ROOM IS...

I'M SORRY.
YOTA, APOLOGIZE TO YOUR AUNT!
HUH?
WHAT'S GOING ON?
RUKA! HOME LATE AGAIN?!
Anyway!
LISTEN TO THIS!
A RENOVATION CREW SHOWED UP TODAY!
We're from Shichikoku Remodeling!
Menu
Finish
I DON'T KNOW ANYTHING ABOUT IT.
I CALLED THEM.
THIS PLACE NEEDS SOME WORK.
YOTA?
YOU MADE THAT DECISION?!
PARDON US! ☆
COMIN' THROUGH!
fump bump
bump—
WHAT?!

I COULDN'T SEE THE WORLD ABOVE...
...FROM THE DARK OCEAN FLOOR.
SIGH
I PROBABLY CAN'T WORK AT HOME TONIGHT.
I'M HOME!
HOW HAVE YOU BEEN RAISING HER?!

Misaki Kamata let me spend half a day observing her doing actual stage makeup and wig styling!

It was fascinating, but I couldn't put much of it in the manga...

Sorry about that, Kamata and Ueki!!

SCENE
38

Yes? Who is it?
ZZT
HELLO, MA'AM ---
BA
IT'S TIME FOR UNILATERAL ACTION!!
WE'RE FROM SHICHI-KOKU REMOD-ELING!
M

...SO WHEN ONE OF US IS OUT OF ACTION, ANOTHER STEPS IN.
THAT'S WHAT WE'VE ALWAYS DONE.
AND RIGHT NOW...
...ONE OF US IS CONFUSED AND STRUG-GLING!
ding dong
Enjoji

WILL YOU MISS ME?
WELL ...
...THIS IS JUST LIKE WORKING ON A MOVIE.
YOU'RE TOGETHER FOR A WHILE...
...AND THEN YOU DISBAND.
YOU CAN'T GO CRYING ABOUT IT.
WE'RE A TEAM...

THEY'RE EASY TO MAKE AND WEAR!
Magnet
Back
Back
HM? DID YOU SAY SOMETHING?
I think I heard you muttering...
NEVER MIND.
LET'S SEE... MAGNETS, MAGNETS...
fwip
Found 'em!
Magnets
OH! POLY-STYRENE FOAM!
IT'S ALREADY OUT!
Lucky me!
...
WAIT. ARE YOU HELP-ING ME?
By any chance?
HUH?
WHO, ME?

HMPH! WHERE'D THEY GO?!
HMM ---
...WHAT SHOULD I USE FOR THESE EAR-RINGS?
Flower Spirit Earrings
RESIN ?
ACRYLIC PLATE?
Umm... Umm...
HEY ---
--- WHERE'S THAT STUFF...
...WE ADD HOT WATER TO?
rustle
Oh!
You mean plastic clay!
GOOD IDEA!
Plastic Clay
Heat to 157°F or higher
glorp
Shape freely
Add color
Use a glue gun!
I CAN SHAPE IT AROUND EARRING POSTS!
ARE THE ACTORS' EARS PIERCED ?
I'LL EMAIL THEM TO FIND OUT!
Group email...
Agh!
THIS MAGNET BROKE.
Must be Tomu's work.
Magnets!
That's even better!

miya Seminar
chatter
chatter
YOTA ENJOJI?
CAN WE TALK?
Tenba Motors
...
WHERE'S EVERY-ONE ELSE?
HM?
UH...

...WE'RE FREE TO TAKE OUR OWN ACTION TOO!
ISN'T THAT RIGHT?
miya Seminar

ALL RIGHT ...
...LET'S DRAW UP A PLAN.
HUH?
RUKA'S FREE WILL IS IMPORTANT...
... BUT ...

WHEN YOU CLOSE YOUR EYES AND GIVE UP...
IZUMI ...
YOU AWAKENED THIS DETERMI-NATION.
... THAT'S WHEN ...
...YOU NEED SOME-ONE'S HELP.

...SHE DOESN'T SEEM LIKE SHE WOULD BE SO DEMANDING!
"DO YOU THINK YOU HAVE NO RIGHT TO SPEAK UP?"
RUKA...
...CAN'T SEE THAT.
"LET ME WORRY ABOUT YOU."
"DON'T YOU KNOW HOW WORRIED I WAS?!"

...IT'S BEST TO AT LEAST GIVE HER SOME GOOD MEMORIES.
Cool!!
Goda's like a hero!!
T-TOMU ...
When did you get here?
I finished training!
GODA IS SACRIFICING HIMSELF FOR SOMEONE ELSE!
LIKE IN A MOVIE!
Right?!
Crying
BUT ...
"RUKA!"
...SUR-PRIS-ING!
RUKA'S MOM!
"I WORRY ABOUT YOU!"
SHE DOESN'T SEEM... YOU KNOW!
??
TOMU, A PROPER SEN-TENCE PLEASE.
WHAT I MEAN IS...

ACCORDING TO RUMOR, IT WAS **GODA** WHO TOLD EVERYONE SHE'S QUITTING!
"TCH! HOWEVER DID THEY FIND OUT?"
HUH?
WHY WOULD HE DO THAT?
I DON'T KNOW FOR SURE, BUT...
...HE PROBABLY THINKS...
...SHE HAS TO MAKE THE DECISION HERSELF.
BEHIND-THE-SCENES WORK TAKES EXTRA-ORDINARY DEDICATION.
AND RUKA IS A CARING PERSON...
...SO HE CAN'T TELL HER TO ABANDON HER STEPMOTHER, WHO'S HAVING A HARD TIME.
THAT'S WHY...

UM, FORGET I SAID ANYTHING!
Y-yeah...
th-thump th-thump
ANYWAY, WORK HARD SO YOU DON'T HAVE REGRETS.
DON'T BE SO HARSH...
THERE!
HERE.
THIS IS FOR CARRYING STUFF. I CALL IT KINJIRO.
You can use it!
KYAHH
No way! It's so unfashionable!
WHAT?! I MADE IT FOR YOU!
It's dreadful!!
WHAT'S GOING ON BETWEEN THOSE TWO?
Are they fighting? Flirting?
Y-YOU WONDER ABOUT THAT TOO?
UH-HUH! I DO!
It's not dreadful!
IF GODA TRIED TO STOP HER FROM QUITTING, SHE MIGHT LISTEN!
I THINK SO TOO!!
Gyaah
Gyaaah
AND GUESS HOW...
...SHE GOT SO MUCH WORK!

Doin' Research Part ③

Scenes 37-38 focus on hairstyling, costumes and props.

I'll... ...do anything!

✧ **Misaki Kamata** ✧

She does a lot of work in 2.5D stage productions.

So I recruited her help!

Blended colors rock!

Black polystyrene foam makes the perfect core for a courtesan's coiffure!

Oyumaru is a good brand!

Plastic clay

She began as a hair stylist. When she had a need for costumes and props, she studied how to make them on her own.

From what I gather, a lot of behind-the-scenes workers are like that. Like stage actors becoming costumers.

YES. SHE SHOWED UP TWO DAYS AGO.
Had a spat with her husband
I'M STAYING AT MY BROTHER'S UNTIL YOU APOLOGIZE!
SHE GOES TO BED EARLY...
9:00 p.m.
Special pillow
RUKA...
...DON'T USE THE SEWING MACHINE AT NIGHT!
...AND SHE'S A LIGHT SLEEPER.
"ARE YOU STILL AWAKE?!"
"WHAT'S ALL THAT STUFF?!"
Kyaaaah
"WE MUST EAT MEALS TOGETHER!"
For shame!
I CAN'T BELIEVE MY BROTHER...
...LET HIS SECOND WIFE RAISE HIS DAUGHTER!
Sigh
I'M AT A LOSS.
I'LL NEVER FINISH IF I DON'T WORK AT HOME.

chirp
chirp
klatter
Ummph!
LET'S GO, DON!
IT'S TIME FOR OUR MORNING-ING JOG!
klatter
Woof
Woof
TOMU...
...LEMME WORK IN THE GARAGE!
5:00 a.m.
I've been waiting!
GACK!!
WHAT?
YOUR MEANEST AUNT...
...IS STAYING AT YOUR HOUSE?!

DID SOMETHING HAPPEN WITH MAIKE?
N-NO, NOTHING! NOTHING AT ALL!
Maike
What a forceful denial...
COULD I, UM, MAYBE HELP OUT?
WOULD YOU?!
THAT WOULD BE A BIG HELP!
OH...
UH, THE ART SQUAD SEEMS BUSY!
Great!!
G-GOOD NIGHT!
WHOOSH
She's so kind...
W-WHAT...?
th-thump
th-thump
WHAT AM I THINKING?!
WAAH

...HAS GIVEN HER CONFIDENCE!
"I HAVE TO GET MARRIED SOON AFTER GRADUATION."
I... ...WASN'T ENOUGH, BUT...
I COULDN'T STOP HER.
SOH?
UM... ...I BROUGHT TEA.
OOPS!
ARE YOU ALL RIGHT?!
YOU'VE BEEN ACTING STRANGELY!
SPLURSH

bwump
FOR A REALISTIC HAIRLINE, I'LL HOOK STRANDS THROUGH THE LACE FRONT.
Before
After
Wow!! It Looks Real!
THEN I CUT AND STYLE IT.
IT'S HEAT RESISTANT, SO I CAN USE A CURLING IRON...
...AND COOL IT AROUND A CYLINDER!
Curly hair.
Heat alone will make it straight
IT HAS TO LOOK REAL...
...WITHIN THE FANTASY WORLD OF THE DRAMA.
CAREFULLY CRAFTED HAIR WILL EXPRESS THE CHARACTER'S ESSENCE.
MOST OF THE BURDEN OF CARRYING THE CHARACTER IS STILL ON THE ACTOR...
...BUT I HELP!
RUKA'S WEALTH OF EXPERIENCE...

HE'S EXTRA HARD ON RUKA.
THERE! ALL READY!
WIGS FOR THE SPIRITS?
YEP!
WHAT ARE THE COLOR STRIPS FOR?
RIGHT NOW, THE WIGS LOOK LIKE THEY'RE FOR A RAVE...
...SO I'LL ADD DEEPER COLORS...
...TO MAKE THEM LOOK MORE NATURAL.
FOR EXAMPLE, IF I ADD DARK GREEN, MILK-TEA BROWN, GRAY AND BEIGE TO A GREEN WIG...
...AND USE A SPONGE TO DARKEN THE ROOTS, IT WILL GAIN DEPTH.

HER FAMILY DECIDED HER FUTURE AND—
RAN-MARU...
...WHAT AM I SUP-POSED TO DO?
THERE IT IS AGAIN.
"ANY-WAY...
...I'M NOT INTER-ESTED."
GODA OFTEN GETS LIKE THIS.
"SOMETIMES MAKING EVERYTHING PERFECT ISN'T NICE."
"I'M NOT INTERESTED IN HEARING YOU CRY!"

Tenba Motors
IT'S TOO MUCH!
RUKA CAN'T HANDLE IT ALL!
THEN SHE CAN REFUSE.
YOU KNOW SHE CAN'T DO THAT!!
AND WE'RE TOO BUSY TO HELP!
TOMU STARTED ACTION SCHOOL, SO WE'RE SHORT-HANDED!
Ruka, it's time!!
Oh, right! We've got meetings!!
THIS IS MAKING HER FINAL DAYS WAY TOO HECTIC!
Waah
Too much to carry!
BE-SIDES...
...AREN'T YOU WORRIED ABOUT HER?!

EACH CHARACTER'S HAIR IS DIFFERENT...
...AND THEIR PROPS NEED ORIGINALITY!
nod
nod
KIMONO? WE DON'T HAVE ENOUGH ON HAND, SO...
...I'LL GET USED KIMONO AND RENTALS.
Film Studies
IT'S A NEAR-FUTURE SUSPENSE!
Uichiro's group
IT'S MUMBLECORE...
...ABOUT A BUNCH OF QUIRKY GIRLS!
Riichi's group
I heard you're quitting?!
A FANTASY ABOUT SPIRITS!
EACH CLAN REPRESENTS SOMETHING, LIKE WOOD, FLOWERS, WIND AND WATER!
THE CLANS HAVE A HIERARCHY, AND EACH CLAN HAS A REPRESENTATIVE COLOR!
WITH A CAST OF 20!
Twenty?! Waah
Theater group: Ptoleminus

DON'T DIE, OKAY?
Turn them down your-self.
FU
MMP
Lethal over-load
IT'S GONNA BE A TUMUL-TUOUS SUMMER !!
You're in command, Ranmaru!
What ?! Me?!
W-what about you?!
You told me to focus on my movie!
IT'S A JAPANESE-STYLE FANTASY!
IT'S GOT A TOKUGAWA SHOGUN-ATE VIBE!
AND 12 AC-TORS!
TAH
DAH
Theater group: Virtual Passage

THEY'RE ALL FOR THE FESTIVAL.
FIVE MOVIES, THREE STAGE PERFORMANCES AND TWO OTHER EVENTS?!
WE'LL NEVER HANDLE ALL THIS!
HM?
COSTUME AND HAIR...
...COSTUME...
...COSTUME AND HAIR AND ART...
...COSTUME...
...HAIR...
COSTUME...
...MORE COSTUME AND HAIR AND ART...
THIS IS ALL FOR RUKA!!
HUH?!
TCH! HOWEVER DID THEY FIND OUT?
EVERYONE HEARD OUR LADY OF THE ART SQUAD IS QUITTING...
Help us!
No, us!!
Huh? But I'm quitting, so...
...I wanted to have fun!
...SO THEY WANT TO DO PROJECTS WITH A FOCUS ON HAIR AND COSTUME.
YEAH, THAT EXPLAINS IT!

I KNOW I SAID GRADU-ATION ...
...BUT THE FESTIVAL IS OUR BIGGEST EVENT.
SO AFTER THE FESTIVAL IS BEST!
I'LL GO OUT WITH A BANG!
B...
BUT...
GODA ALREADY AGREED.
GOOD! YOU'RE ALL HERE!
WE'VE GOT NEW JOBS!
FU
MPP
HUH?
WHAT IS ALL THIS?!

It happened right before summer vacation.
I'M QUITTING AFTER THE SCHOOL FESTIVAL IN OCTOBER.

Behind the Scenes!! Slip-Up
The Kurisu family got shut out!!
Oh dear!
SOB
We just show our heads in this volume!
Dad is distraught!!
I planned to show Ranmaru going home for New Year's, but the story skips from Christmas to spring, so...
Sorry...
Ah, my regret!

SCENE
37

POOM
THE FIRE-WORKS...
...ARE ALMOST OVER.

YOU AWAKENED THIS DETERMINATION.
Wahoo!
I HOPE ...
...RUKA IS ALL RIGHT.
Enjoji

All right. Off you go!
EVEN IF IT ALL ENDS IN FAILURE...
...THERE'S STILL A POINT IN TRYING.
EVEN IF YOU WERE HER MOTIVATION...
...IZUMI.

POOM

THE FIRE-WORKS ...

THAT LOOKS PAIN-FUL...
...BUT YOU'RE HOLDING UP WELL!
YOU'RE REALLY DOING GREAT!
FWEE~
HM?

THIS SHOULD GET YOU THROUGH.
I...
...BROUGHT AN EXTRA BELT CORD.
RAN...
SHOW ME YOUR FEET, SOH.

WHAT A COINCIDENCE! ☆
I CAME TOO! WITH MY BOYFRIEND! ♡
Is she bragging?!
OH, IT'S MAASA.
HEY, MAIKE!
I'M GLAD WE RAN INTO YOU, SOH!
HAVE YOU GOT A SEC?
IT'S ABOUT WHAT WE TALKED ABOUT!
HUH? THE FIREWORKS ARE GOING TO START!
She'll be right back! ☆
??
SH
MAKE IT FAST, RAN-MARU!!
SOH! LIFT YOUR ARMS!!

LET'S GET SOH AND GO.
SHE CAN'T HANDLE ANY—
NO...
FOR HER SAKE...
...SEE THIS THROUGH TO THE END!!
...
OH! HI, SOH!

WHAT SHOULD I DO?
pang pang
MY FEET HURT...
RUKA TOLD ME TO GET USED TO WEARING THESE...
...BUT MY MIND WAS ON OTHER THINGS.
slip
THIS IS...
...NO GOOD.
IT'S NOT FAIR TO MAIKE...
...THAT I'M THIS TENSE DURING OUR DATE.
RAN-MARU...

Waist string.
Under belt.
I CAN BARELY BREATHE!
THE WAIST STRING IS TOO TIGHT!
SKWEEN SKWEEN
KOBORA?
AM I WALKING TOO FAST?
Sorry!
N-NO, NOT AT ALL!
I THINK I CAN STRUGGLE THROUGH ...
SLIP
But my belt is coming loose!!!
DADUM
I NEED A REST-ROOM ...
Not gonna happen.

Doin' Research Part ②

And this showed up in storage!

The Monster!!
Master-piece!!
Urethane foam foundation
+
colored liquid rubber

I wanted the manga to include a bit about making a monster, but it wouldn't fit.

Ah, my regret!

The video of the superhero show at the school festival is a ✧masterpiece!✧ Check out the official website!!

Thank you so much to...

The Monster Association at Waseda University!!

"SOME THINGS ARE JUST INEVITA-BLE."
"I CAN'T DO ANYTHING ABOUT IT."
HM?

THEY FOUND A GOOD SPOT.
DO YOU MIND WALKING A LITTLE?
HUH? WE'RE GONNA JOIN YOUR FRIENDS?!
DOES THAT MAKE YOU NER-VOUS?
HA HA! I DIDN'T KNOW YOU WERE SHY!
DON'T WORRY! IT'LL BE FINE!!
BE MORE CONSID-ERATE!!!
Shyness is no joke!
Whoa!
SHE LOOKS DETER-MINED.
SOH...
...

Ugh...
OH NO...
THIS AREA WAS WIDE OPEN LAST YEAR!
LOOK OVER THERE!
GLOOM
THERE'S NO ONE OVER THERE, BUT...
Is that my name?!
Soh
WHOA ...
Worked hard all day.♥
Don't do as Maasa does.
THAT PLACE IS CURSED. LET'S GO SOME-WHERE ELSE.
NO! YOU IDIOTS !!
tomp tomp
ting♪
SORRY. IT'S FROM SOME FRIENDS.
THEY'RE HERE TOO.
OH.

GETTING FOOD ON YOUR YUKATA AND KILLING THE MOOD!!!
MP P
I CAUGHT AN OCTOPUS!!
CHO
Takoyaki
Ta
BE MORE CAREFUL, PUNK!
Or an evil clown will get you!
?
Where'd it go?
?
clomp clomp
NO RUN-NING!
YOU'LL GET SAUCE ON SOME-ONE!!
clomp
clomp
EX-AMPLE 2!
FIGHT-ING FOR A SEAT!!
crowded

I'M GLAD SHE GOT HER KIMONO ON!!
Shichikoku University Station (North)
SOH LOOKS GOR-GEOUS!!
AND THEY FOUND EACH OTHER ---
--- WITHOUT ANY DIFFI-CULTY!
WHICH MEANS WE'RE DONE HERE, SO—
NOT SO FAST!
THIS IS JUST GETTING STARTED!
HUH?
FIRE-WORKS DATES CARRY MANY RISKS!
EXAM-PLE 1!!
Takoyaki
Cotton Candy
tump tump ba-tump
BUMP
KYAH!

chatter
Shichikoku Town Fireworks
Ako Tea
Choco
$2.00
chatter
KOBORA!!
MAIKE!
S-SORRY I'M LATE!
NO PROBLEM.
I'M GLAD YOU CAME.
I'M JUST LUCKY TO GET A DATE...
...SINCE YOU REFUSED AT FIRST.
SO THANKS.
YOU LOOK GREAT IN A YUKATA.

I'LL FIGURE IT OUT MYSELF!!
SHE REALLY WANTS MATCHING OUTFITS!
SOH, ARE YOU ALL RIGHT?!
C-CAN I HELP YOU?!
Stay out!
I'm concentrating!!
THE GIRL'S GOT METTLE!
YOUR USELESSNESS HAS AWAKENED HER DETERMINATION.
HUH? THIS IS MY FAULT?
ACTUALLY, I DIDN'T FULLY REALIZE.

RUKA ?
I CAN'T GO!
A BUNCH OF RELATIVES CAME OVER!
THE'RE GOING TO WATCH THE FIREWORKS FROM THE TERRACE! BUT NO ONE TOLD ME!
RUKA ---
PLEASE, VISIT WITH OUR GUESTS.
MAKE ME LOOK GOOD, OKAY?
HUH ?
UM ---
Waaah!
Sorry!
CAN ANYONE ELSE HELP SOH CHANGE?
I CAN TIE A BOY'S, BUT...
Soh's mom
SOH, YOU'LL HAVE TO WEAR WESTERN CLOTHES!
Like a jumper.
I DON'T HAVE A CLUE !!
Sorry!
I CAN'T !
MAIKE'S COMING IN A YUKATA!
HMF

blah
FIRE-WORKS MAKE USE OF SOMETHING CALLED FLAME REACTION.
blah blah
LOOK. THIS IS A CHRYSAN-THEMUM ...
...AND THIS IS A PEONY ...
Chrysanthemum
Peony
...AND THIS IS A GREAT WILLOW.
Great Willow
THIS'LL BE A GREAT TOPIC...
...FOR CONVER-SATION!
Don't thank me.
Hey, Riku!
SHE DOESN'T NEED ALL THAT INFORMA-TION!!!
SHE JUST NEEDS TO SAY, "OOH! HOW PRETTY!"
Why is Izumi here?!
Yikes
Yikes
SORRY ABOUT THE OTHER DAY, SOH.
GOOD LUCK WITH YOUR DATE!!
This is a palm tree!
Why is Izumi wishing me luck?!
IS HE BULLY-ING ME?!
YOU SHOULD PUT ON YOUR YUKATA.
BUT RUKA ISN'T HERE!
I PICKED IT UP YESTER-DAY, BUT...
Ruka Art Squad
tingaling

RUKA ---
AND I'LL HELP YOU PUT IT ON! ♡
WE COULD BLEND IN WITH THE CROWD ---
Poof Poof
Nuh-uh!
SWIK
Good
WE'RE READY TO GO!!
YOU'RE GONNA SPY ON HER?!
The day of Soh's date...
GOT IT, SOH?
RED COMES FROM STRONTIUM CARBONATE...
--- BLUE IS FROM COPPER OXIDE ---
...AND GOLD IS FROM TITANIUM.
Kya ha ha
ha ha
ha

WE'LL MEET IN THE EVENING...
...AND HAVE FESTIVAL FOOD...
Bento
Unnecessary
No buttons
...AND HE'S GOING TO WEAR A YUKATA.
Ah ha ha!
Tee hee hee!
Objective achieved:
Matching Outfits
(sort of)
It was all for nothing...
BUT I PRACTICED SO HARD!
GOD!!!
You saved herrr!
Hmf
FIRE-WORKS DISPLAY DATE PLANS...
mutter mutter
She switched modes!
HEY, SOH?
DO YOU KNOW HOW TO WEAR A KIMONO?
Gasp
UH... NO.
I DON'T EVEN HAVE ONE!! IT'S SHOPPING TIME!
FWOOOSH!
Wait! I'll Lend you one!

"LOOK FOR A CHANCE TO CALL HIM 'MAIKE BABY' OR 'RUIHEI DARLING.'"
Nickname
Ruihei Maike
Michael ✕
Too normal
Maicheru ✕
Rui-Rui ✕
Not awful
Jack Son
Trademarked?
FIRST, SHE NEEDS A SENSE OF SHAME!
I DOUBT SHE'D ACTUALLY DO IT, BUT...
Whoa...
SOH CAN HANDLE THIS!
NEVER UNDERESTIMATE HER!
SHE'S CAN BE OBSESSIVELY SINGLE-MINDED!!
Practice bento by Soh ☆
WHICH IS WHY YOU GOTTA HELP HER!
WAAAAAAAHH
She's gonna...
...get hurrrrt!
RANMARU, YOU'VE TOTALLY FORFEITED YOUR ROLE AS HER COUSIN.
OH NO... WHAT SHOULD WE DO?
Ping
SOH, YOU GOT MAIL.
IT'S FROM MAIKE!!
IT'S A DATE PLAN!
IN A FEW DAYS...
...HE WANTS TO WATCH FIREWORKS.

SOH, DO YOU REALLY WANT TO BE SUCH A DUMB COUPLE?
This could ruin the date!
WERE YOU ALWAYS SO METICULOUS?
Y-YES! WHAT SHOULD I DO?!
SOH! IT'S TOO SOON FOR MATCHING OUTFITS!!
RANMARU, YOU'RE OVER-REACTING.
SOH, IF YOU DON'T WANT TO GET SERIOUS...
...THEN...
This is too much.
WAAAH
DON'T TALK TO ME!!
YOU'LL DISTURB MY BUTTON-SEWING!!!
S-sorry...
FWIP
WHY WOULD HE LOSE A BUTTON?
WILL HIS CLOTHES EVEN HAVE BUTTONS?
Hmm...
THERE'S MORE WRITTEN HERE.
"In the worst case scenario, rip off a button."
BRUTE FORCE?!

Today
Don't mess up!!
Perfect Date Plan No. 5
• Matching outfits
Ask what Maike's going to wear.
Casually!
• Feed him parfait, etc.
Get cream around his mouth on purpose.
You can do it!
Optimum angle: 47.2°.
Could be tough!
• If a button comes off, sew it back on.
• Let him rest his head in your lap. / Have him lift you in his arms.
• Use pet names like "baby," "darling," and "honey."
• Coquettish klutziness
Fall down,
RANMARU TOOK A PIC OF SOH'S IDEAL DATE PLAN.
BUT...
Tenba Moto
WHAT?!
Soh's Notebook
THIS WILL BE A DISASTER!!!
HMF
Practicing sewing on buttons

ACTUALLY, I DON'T CARE.
Is it fun filming this?
Pay me no mind.
DO YOU WONDER WHAT YOU WERE LIKE BEFORE YOUR MEMORY LOSS?
OH...
WELL, SORT OF.
IN THE PAST, I WISHED I KNEW WHAT I WAS LIKE BEFORE...
...BUT WHEN I FELL IN THE FOREST...
...I HAD A STRANGE SENSATION...
...I CAN'T DE-SCRIBE.
Ah ha ha
BUT... AW, WHO KNOWS!
OH.
I GUESS I MADE SOH ANGRY.
shf
WANT A CHANCE TO MAKE IT UP?
LOOK AT THIS.

I TRACE THE PATTERN FROM THE POTTERY ...
...AND THEN CREATE A NEW PATTERN.
LIKE THIS.
CHANGING THE ARRANGE-MENT IS INTER-ESTING.
I WONDER WHAT IT WAS LIKE BEFORE?
I don't know.
Behind the Scenes!! Slip-Up
Did Soh Kobora skip a grade?
Huh ?!
When Soh first appeared, the manga said she was in year 2 of high school, but later it was year 3.
Sorry... I wanted her and Ranmaru to be one year apart, so "Year 2" was a mistake. I think.

SCENE
36

THERE WASN'T MUCH TRAFFIC.
AND THAT'S WHERE I FELL.
BUT ...
...WHY DID I FALL?

...I'M GONNA GO ON A DATE WITH MAIKE!!
HUH ?!
HUH?
rub
BUT ...
And I'm GONNA eat a parfait !!
WHAAAT?!
THE VIEW WAS NICE FROM UP THERE.

SOH !!
DID YOU GET A GOOD VIDEO?
When did you start filmimg?
VR R—
IT'S NOT BAD.
SOH!
DON'T RUN! IT'S DANGER-OUS!
OH...
...WHO CARES !!
WHOOSH
I'M TIRED OF THIS!
I WANT TO FOR-GET IT ALL!
SO...

...IS SO FUNNY?!
DON'T YOU KNOW HOW WORRIED I WAS?!
YOU FELL BECAUSE YOU'RE ALWAYS SPACING OUT AND NOT PAYING ATTENTION!
WHY?!
THE REST OF YOU TOO!
THIS IS SERI-OUS...
...SO WHY...
SOH...

DID I...
...FALL AGAIN?
HM?
DID YOUR MEMORY RETURN ?
NOPE! NOT A THING! ☆
AH HA HA HA HA HA
Well, at least he isn't hurt.
FOR A MOMENT, I WONDERED THOUGH!
UGH!!
WHAT ...

IZUMI !!
IZUMI?!
WHAT HAPPENED?!
IZUMI!!
CALL AN AMBULANCE!
OW...
OUCH...
IZUMI!!

"HE'S SUFFERING FROM AMNESIA DUE TO THE ACCIDENT."
"WHY DID HE...
...FALL FROM THERE?"

A BUTTER-FLY...
W...
WAAAH!

tump
tump
AFTER GRAD-UATION ...
...HE PLANS TO TRAVEL AROUND.
MAYBE HE WANTS TO FIND HIMSELF.
I DON'T KNOW IF HE'LL ABANDON EVERY-THING...
...BUT ...
...I DON'T THINK HE INTENDS TO COME BACK.

...PASSES RIGHT THROUGH.
DADUMM
HUH? I THOUGHT THAT WAS A SHORTCUT, BUT...
Lost
Spshh (Water)
THIS WAY?
rustle rustle
HUH?!
IZUMI HASN'T COME BACK?!
What's that airhead up to?!
SPLIT UP AND SEARCH!
SOH! COME WITH ME!
SOH...?
Hey, Izumi!

EVERYONE CARES ABOUT YOU, SO...
UM, IZUMI WENT UPSTREAM.
HE'S JUST LIKE...
...A TRANSPARENT PIECE OF GLASS.
PRETTY...
...BUT EVERYTHING...

MAIKE SEEMS...
...LIKE A NICE GUY.
HE SEEMS DEPENDABLE.
Shichikoku Handsome Dude Cont
Q1 What were you like as a chi
Q2 What was your dream a
Q3 Who was your favorite
Q4 What ju
"I'M SURPRISED...
...AT HOW FEW ANSWERS I HAVE."
IZUMI...
...DO YOU LIKE ANYONE?
DOES YOUR MEMORY LOSS WORRY YOU?
IS THERE ANYTHING I CAN DO?
I WANT TO HELP.
AND IT'S NOT JUST ME.

THERE MAY BE MORE UPSTREAM.
MAYBE THERE WAS A KILN NEAR-BY...
...OR A SETTLE-MENT.
IZUMI ---
...WHAT ARE YOUR PLANS AFTER GRADU-ATION?
Huh?
SORRY. I WASN'T LISTENING.
Did you say some-thing?
N-NO...
... NEVER MIND.

D...
DID YOU FIND ANYTHING GOOD?
YEAH.
LOOK.
POTTERY FRAG-MENTS?
YOU CAN STILL SEE THE DESIGN.
I CAN MAKE A GOOD PATTERN WITH THESE.

WOW --- HE'S LIKE A DIF-FERENT PER-SON!
He's good with his hands!
COOL!
TEACH ME!
Ugh!
This is hard! You're impres-sive!!
What a great guy...
Let's decorate them!
With leaves and sticks!
Oooh!
Whoa!!
Are you going to action school?!
Yup!!
I just started!

THIS THING.
OH, I'VE SEEN THOSE ON TV!
How nice! ♡
I could use one to hang a lantern! ♡
O... OKAY!
SHARPEN THE END THAT GOES IN THE GROUND FOR STABILITY!
GR
ND
O... OKAY!
YOU'D BE WISE TO LEARN ROPE-WORK!
OKAY !!

CHECK THIS OUT.
VRRR
Moves automatically
AND THIS!
VRR—R
IT REDUCES SHAKING FOR SMOOTH FILMING!
SMOO—TH
W... WOW!!
YOU COULD MAKE A MOVIE WITH THAT!!
Have you started?
WHICH REMINDS ME...
TUMP
I'M STILL BRAIN-STORM-ING.
First, I need to mas-ter this camera.
CHIEF!!
WILL THESE THICK STICKS WORK?
YEAH, THEY'RE PER-FECT!
RANMARU, USE THEM TO MAKE TRIPODS.
I'm on camera duty!
TRI-WHAT?

IT SOUNDS SO IMPOSSIBLE!
GYAIIEEE
clik clik
WHOA. YOU MAKE IT SOUND LIKE A MISSION.
D...
DID YOU BUY THAT?
Oh!
YEP!!
A TRIAXIAL ELECTRIC STABILIZER!!
Doin' Research Part 1
For Tomu's story in Scene 34...
The Monster Association at Waseda University
...gave me some help!!
High-quality...
...hand-made costume!
peel
Velcro makes changing parts easy!
WOW!
This is Kugutsuko!
Kugutsuko! How cute!
She's even got a cool backstory!

W...
WHAT ARE YOU DOING?!
I NEED TO KNOW HOW SERIOUS HE IS!
THIS CALLS FOR A BOLD CON-FRON-TATION!!
th-thmp th-thmp
No, don't!! I told you I turned him down!!
But I didn't exactly refuse a date!
DATE?!
I...I thought once couldn't hurt!
B...
But...
DO YOU EVEN KNOW WHAT A DATE IS?!
Y...
Yes!
chuckle
You share the same parfait!
AND RUN ALONG THE BEACH...
...AND FROLIC IN THE SEA!
giggle
Gasp
But who pays?!
GACK
Do we split it?!
When do I get out my wallet?!
BUT WHAT IF HE WANTS TO PAY TO LOOK GOOD?!
You mean I might offend him?!
GACK

"I'M SORRY."
...SOH STILL LIKES IZUMI.
SOH!! IZUMI'S SO COOL!
HUH?
Y-YEAH, BUT...
HE'S QUIET AND MATURE! ♡♡
BUT ...
...YOUR COUSIN IS SORTA JITTERY.
jitter
jitter
Oh, you like snow-boarding and surfing?
jitter
...
Uh-huh

BUT ...
Come join us!
No! I'm fine!
Soh, this meat is done.
Oh, thanks!
Izumiii!
How should we polish this?
I recommend a diamond file!
Gradually use finer files...
...while applying water.

AT FIRST, IT WAS NO BIG DEAL.
A FRIEND INVITED ME TO HELP WITH HER CLUB.
I DIDN'T KNOW ANYTHING ABOUT PERFORMING OR WORKING BEHIND THE SCENES...
...AND IT WAS HARDER THAN I EXPECTED.
BUT...
...IT REALLY TOUCHED MY HEART.
What a sweet guy!
This meat tastes awesome!
PSST PSST
HE JUST NATURALLY DEVEL-OPED A CRUSH?!
Or was that your goal?
HE LOOKS LIKE THE POPULAR TYPE!
HOW SERI-OUS IS IT?!
WHAT'S HE LIKE IN DAILY LIFE? DOES HE HAVE A PLAN FOR THE FUTURE?
WHAT ARE YOU? HER MOTHER?

BECAUSE HE'S TOTALLY INTO SOH!
What kind of mush-rooms do you like?
Shiitake...
Oh! Me too!!
HE TOLD HER HE LIKES HER, BUT...
SOH...
...HAS A SUITOR ?!
Is it t-true, Soh?!
Eep! This is so embar-rassing!
But I turned him down!!
Huh? Really?

HE'S LIKE A FAWNING PUPPY!
Which is okay!
A younger man is okay!!
UM, BUT...
MAASA, DID YOU BRING YOUR NOTEBOOKS...
...FULL OF YOUR POEMS ABOUT LOVE RAGE?
THE ONES CURSING BOYS FROM THE COUNTLESS SINGLES PARTIES YOU'VE ATTENDED!
YOU SAID THEY WERE PILING UP!
You confuse me
With false sweetness
And ripe dark poison
You should die!
Die and die!
You mock me
My Hades
Listen to me
Y...
Plunge to Purgatory!
Hell!
Hell!!
in a space
C'MON! WE'LL ADD THEM TO THE FIRE!
YOU IDIOT!
BUT YOU SAID YOU'RE HUNGRY LIKE A WOLF FOR MEN AND NEED TO PURIFY YOURSELF OF—
YEAH, BUT DON'T YOU HAVE ANY DISCRETION?!
HUH?
Gasp
g...grin
W...
WE FEEL YOU. WE WERE EYEING HIM TOO...
...BUT HE'S A LOST CAUSE.
Kobora, can I assist you?
gush gush

I GOT WATER FROM THE WELL!!
WHERE SHOULD I PUT IT?
Ruihei Maike (18)
Year 1, Mashubon University
Oh no!!
HE LOOKS LIKE HE JUST STEPPED OUT OF A FASHION MAGAZINE!!
S...
SORRY! HE'S WITH ME!
I WAS TALKING ABOUT THE BARBE-QUE AND...
"CAN I COME ALONG?"
He helps the drama club!
Heh heh heh
THAT'S OKAY. AT FIRST HE STRUCK ME AS THE FRIVOLOUS TYPE I CAN'T STAND, BUT...
Thank you for letting me come!!
HE'S SUPER-POLITE!
Please! Take a window seat!!
AND CONSID-ERATE!
Don't trouble your-self!!
I'll carry these!!
Ooh!
THOSE LOOK DELI-CIOUS!
MAASA PRE-PARED THEM!
Food for baking in tinfoil!!
YOU DON'T SAY!
Wow!
MAASA! LET'S BAKE THEM RIGHT AWAY!

UM, CHIEF?
I BORROWED A GRILL, SO PRIMITIVE MEASURES AREN'T NECESSARY.
RAN-MARU, YOU'RE TOO SOFT!
YOU'D NEVER SURVIVE IN THE WILD!
S-sorry!
YOU GREW UP BY THE SEA, BUT YOU CAN'T BUILD A FIRE?!
WHAT A FINELY WROUGHT SHAPE!
HOW MANY EONS HAS THIS PEBBLE SEEN?
GO INTO RAPTURES OVER THE FATHOMLESS HISTORY OF MOTHER NATURE LATER!
It's meat time!
L...
LET US HELP!
SORRY! WE TAGGED ALONG WITH SOH!
Soh and Friends from the Kokuto University Theater Circle
THAT'S FINE! THE MORE THE MER-RIER!
Yeah.
THE BOYS ARE THE ONES WHO SHOULD APOLO-GIZE!
BUT WHO HAVE WE HERE?
SORRY I'M LATE!!

...EVERY-THING'S READY FOR THE BAR-BECUE!
WE ALL...
...THREW A BARBECUE.

BUILD STABLE WALLS WITH ROCKS...
...LEAVING GAPS FOR AIR TO ENTER...
...WHICH WILL CAUSE HEAT TO ACCUMULATE AT THE CONFLUENCE.
YOU CAN POLISH AGATES...
...OR ADMIRE THEM IN THE ROUGH.
AND YOU CAN MAKE THEM INTO MAGNETS...
...OR USE WIRE TO FASHION A PENDANT FROM THEM.
ALL RIGHT...
...YOU SURVIVALISTS AND DREAMERS...

LISTEN UP...
LOOK! STRIPES!
...THE MOST IMPORTANT PART OF BUILDING A FIRE IS AIRFLOW.
IT MUST BE AN AGATE!
BAM

I HAD BEEN WAIT-ING...
...SO LONG...
...FOR THAT MO-MENT.

Behind the Scenes of Behind the Scenes!! 1

Behind the Scenes!! has benefited from lots of talent behind the scenes! I could never have written this manga without the help of the art staff.

↓ Congrats!

← Behind the Scenes!! Good work completing the series!

This is the background specialist and woman in charge of humming. She's enthusiastic, but she's often injured.

The story about Izumi burning his hand came from her real life.

Yui Natsuki
夏生ゆい

Team☆Hatori's longest-serving member and its brains!!

She has a full grasp of all the art supplies and screentones.

Aya designed most of Ranmaru's and Tomu's T-shirts.

And she's an entertainer who does bad impressions!

Aya Aomura
碧村綾

Ranmaru and Grinyan T-shirt

Good work, Bisco!! ↑

SCENE
35

• 00:01:03
...that the whole group had taken a step forward.
This moment belonged to them all.

th-thmp
That day...
...some-thing awakened within Tomu.
00:00
Time Lapse Slow Video
He realized ...

You were great, Tomu!
So dashing!
Heh heh!
OH!
I'M ...
Camera check
...JUMPING TOO HIGH...
...AND NOT IN SYNC WITH THE OTHERS.
IF I CONTROL MYSELF, THE HERO WILL STAND OUT MORE.
NEXT TIME...
th-thmp
...I SHOULD BE MORE ...

And then...
... filming began.
SMC X SF
3-2

...I CAN BE A HERO TOO!
Huh?!
YOU'RE GONNA BE A COSTUME ACTOR?!
I HADN'T THOUGHT OF THAT!
W...
Wow, Tomu!!
Does that mean...
YOU'RE GONNA WEAR THE SHICHI-COCOON Z COSTUME I MADE?!
Yay!
WHOA!
That Looks cool!!
ACTUALLY, I'M GONNA PLAY SHOCKER.
Heh heh
Huh?
Ugh...
I need to teach him to stay in frame...
Camera Test

I'VE ALWAYS ADMIRED THEM...
...AND IMAGINED THEM EXISTING IN ANOTHER WORLD.
BUT NOW...
...THEY'RE SOMETHING MORE...
AND WE HAVE A CONNECTION...
...SO MAYBE...

STAY IN FORMA-TION!
AND BE AWARE OF YOUR SUR-ROUND-INGS!
THIS ISN'T JUST ABOUT YOU!
SUPER-HERO ACTION REQUIRES TEAM COORDI-NATION!!
HEROES ALWAYS FIGHT FOR OTHERS.

HE EVEN WANTED TO BE AN ACTION STAR.
RUN!!
WH
SH
SKIP!!
JUMP!!
SOMER-SAULT!!
HEY! THIS IS EASY!
UMPP
B
OOF!
Grah! Blond-ie!!!

PEOPLE DO THAT?!
Go talk to him.
Thought heroes were just heroes
TOMU WOULD BE A GREAT COSTUME ACTOR.
BUT I WONDER WHEN HE'LL NOTICE.
PRO-FES-SOR...
...HE'S IN THE ART SQUAD!
And he's dumb!
ALL RIGHT!! LET'S START WITH BASIC ACTIONS!!
Hm?
WHAT?
Whah?! Huh?!
Dance Club
Gymnastics Club
Recruited for the cast.☆
Yeah.
THE PRO-FESSOR'S AN SFX NUT.

YOU'LL BE A SUPER-HERO!
THE MAN BEHIND THE MASK!
P...

Hey!
YOU'RE THE OLD GUY ON THE BENCH!
THAT'S RIGHT.
WHAT'S PARKOUR?
YOU DON'T KNOW?
Why are we here?
I'M NOT JUST AN OLD GUY.
I'M A PRO-FES-SOR.
Gymnasium
AND ...
...I ADVISE THE SFX MOVIE CLUB.
I WANT YOU ...
...TO BE IN OUR MOVIE!
WHAT?

Greetings

This is *Behind the Scenes!!* volume 7!! The final volume!!

Thank you...
...very much!!

The final volume turned out to be rushed and crammed with content (even more than usual).

Anyway... it was decided a while back that volume 7 would conclude the series.

Chock-full Plans

Will all this fit?

In a slump
Hm? I can't get...
...this layout right!

But I gave it my all!! I hope you like it!!

HEY, BLONDIE!
YOU WERE DOING PARKOUR IN THE PARK THE OTHER DAY, WEREN'T YOU?
YOU'RE A STUDENT AT SHICHI-KOKU, RIGHT?
COME WITH ME.
HUH?!

...HE'S CUT OUT FOR MORE!

A LOT OF PEOPLE LIVE THAT WAY.
BUT I THINK...

OH WELL...
I'M SURE HE'LL BE BACK SOON...
...BECAUSE HE BOUNCES BACK EASILY.
AND HE DOES HAVE HIS STRENGTHS.
HUH?
HE THINKS HE CAN'T DO ANYTHING.
HE'S DOESN'T REALIZE IT...
...BUT HE'S ABLE TO KEEP LAUGHING BECAUSE HE DOESN'T EXPECT MUCH FROM HIMSELF...
...AND THAT'S A KIND OF STRENGTH.
Gasp
I SHOULD HEAD BACK.
Uh-oh... The drinks aren't cold anymore!
Oh well!
ISN'T MAASA GONNA GET A JOB MAKING ZOMBIES?
I'LL JUST HELP DAD AT THE SHOP...
...BUT SHE HAS POTENTIAL!

SO I WANTED TO HELP, BUT...
...I REALLY...
...CAN'T DO ANYTHING!
GUYS!
HE ISN'T ANSWERING!
BVVVT
BVVVT
HE DIDN'T TAKE HIS PHONE.
It's over here.
AGH!
OH NO... MAYBE I WAS TOO HARD ON HIM.
BUT HE WAS SO EXCITED...
HE REALLY FLIPS OUT OVER SUPERHEROES.
I totally ridiculed him!
BUT WHEN HE HELPS, IT'S A DISASTER!
Even worse...
Oh! So this isn't poop?
HAHA
HA
Tomu...

ba Motors
HM?
WHERE'S TOMU?
THOSE GUYS...
...ARE SO COOL.
I'VE ALWAYS ...
...BELIEVED THAT HEROES ACTUALLY EXIST IN REAL LIFE.

splop
...
OH! HARD AT WORK?
WHATCHA MAKIN', TOMU? A PILE OF POOP?
Lookin' Good!
Tomu's Dad
※ Former Thug
...

ALL RIGHT. START WITH THE CLAY.
WAHOOOOOO
glorp
UM... DO YOU WANT ME TO DO IT?
Paper pattern
RRIP
SLAP
TOMU... DO YOU WANT ME TO TAKE OVER?
T-Tomu! Use a utility knife!
CRACK
It's scary how you hold that!!
No blades for you!
Weren't you making the same shape?
Tomu's
TOSS
I wanna do it!
I wanna do it!
I wanna do it!
Clay
W...
WELL, THERE'S SOME EXTRA CLAY.
S...
SO MAKE ROUND BALLS OR SOME-THING.

AND THE ARMOR NEEDS TO BE REMOVABLE!
SO MAKE A PROTOTYPE WITH THICK PAPER...
...TO SERVE AS A BASIS FOR THE URETHANE FOAM.
Graph paper.
G10
Urethane foam.
Use a firm sponge inside to give it bulk.
Finish by applying a lustrous fabric.
Under-side.
Use metal or wooden sticks.
Decorate sneakers
EASILY INTER-CHANGEABLE ELEMENTS MAKES FOR A PRETTY COOL TRICK! ☆
Transformation!!
Inter-changeable elements!
Velcro
FRIP
I WANNA DO IT!! LEMME DO IT!!
Yaay Yaay~

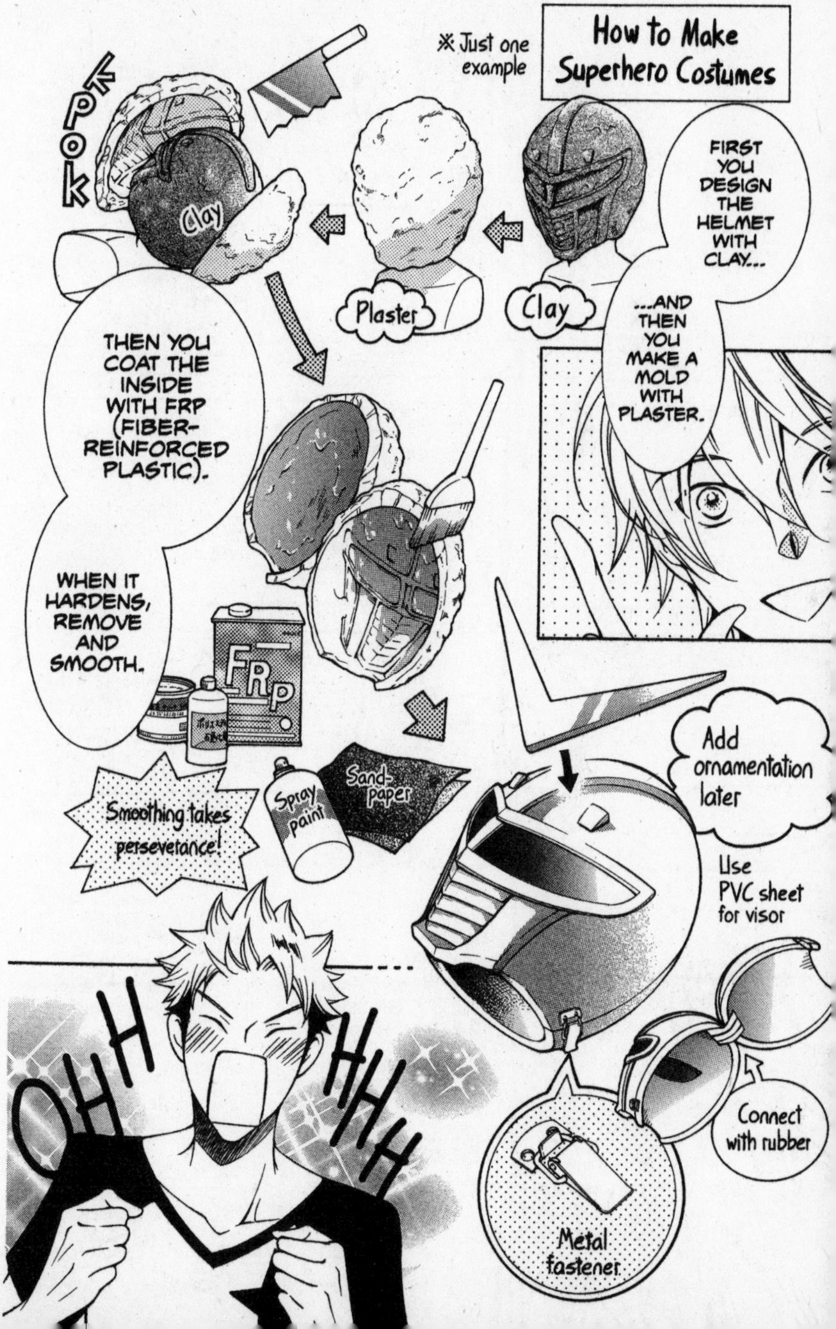
How to Make Superhero Costumes
※Just one example
FIRST YOU DESIGN THE HELMET WITH CLAY...
Clay
Plaster
...AND THEN YOU MAKE A MOLD WITH PLASTER.
Clay
Pok
THEN YOU COAT THE INSIDE WITH FRP (FIBER-REINFORCED PLASTIC).
WHEN IT HARDENS, REMOVE AND SMOOTH.
FRP
Add ornamentation later
Use PVC sheet for visor
Smoothing takes perseverance!
Spray paint
Sand-paper
Connect with rubber
Metal fastener
OHHHHHH

BE-SIDES, YOUR CHAR-ACTER SKETCH...
...LOOKS LIKE A KINDER-GAR-TENER'S DOO-DLE!
And it's not cool!
Sh...
SHUT UP! Anyway, you skipped the meet-ing!!
URGH
I HAD A JOB-HUNTING WORK-SHOP!
You nincompoop!
I'M LOOKING FOR A COMPANY FULL OF HANDSOME DUDES!!
LET'S JUST DO THE BEST WE CAN!
I'VE ALWAYS WANTED TO MAKE A SUPERHERO COSTUME.
MAYBE I'LL MAKE THE MAIN ONE...
fidget
NO, YOU'RE IN A SUPPORTIVE ROLE FOR THIS.
DIRECTING YOUR MOVIE IS OF UTMOST IMPORTANCE!
AND I'VE BEEN WAITING FOREVER!
You're stubborn...
C'mon, let me do it!
It sounds fun!
Nope! Don't bother!
I LOOKED UP HOW TO MAKE THEM.
RANMARU, SHOULD WE USE FRP FOR THE HELMETS?
Y...
YES, GOOD IDEA!
AND URETHANE FOAM FOR THE BODY!
Polyester Hardener

GWOOO
YOU UNDER-ESTIMATE MY LOVE OF SUPER-HEROES!
I CAN MAKE AN ARMY OF THEM!
AND THEY'LL BE SO COOL IT KILLS YOU!!
GIVE ME A BREAK!
HOW STUPID ARE YOU?
WE'VE NEVER DONE THIS BEFORE!
YOU SHOULD'VE GIVEN IT MORE THOUGHT...
...BEFORE GETTING A BIG HEAD AND ACCEPTING THE JOB!

Shichikoku Warrior
Shichicocoon Z
This is a true super-hero!!
After Eclosion
Light Warrior Shichi-cocoon Z!!!
Silkworm Gun
Silkworm Shuriken
A MOTH THEME?!
Where's the deeper mean-ing?
Right! He's a Light Warrior!
Light attracts moths, so...
Why is a cook bad...
...but a moth is okay?!
I WANT THE ART SQUAD TO MAKE COSTUMES...
Psycho Shogun
...FOR THE MAIN HERO AND FOUR VILLAINS...
...BUT IS THAT ASKING TOO MUCH?
WELL, FOUR IS QUITE A LOT...

TA DA
HOW ABOUT SHICHI-COOK-MAN NO. 16?!
CHECK IT OUT.
Shichicook-Man No. 16
Good at making rice omelets.
Fork-shaped Machine Gun
16
Strong
Rocket Punch
HIS CATCH-PHRASE IS "I'LL ADD YOUR EVIL TO MY SOUP!"
AAH
UM... WHAT?
YOU CAN USE MY SUPERHERO IDEA!!
TOMU...
Um...
WHY SHICHI-COOK?
CUZ IT SOUNDS LIKE SHICHKOKU!!
H
WHY NO. 16?
BECAUSE OF MY NAME!!
To Mu
10+6
IT'S A FLIMSY IDEA!
AND IT LACKS ALL DEEPER MEANING!
Snicker
OHHHH

Light Warrior
Production Meeting
THE MOVIE!
SF
GEN-TLE-MEN!
WE HERE AT SHICHI-KOKU UNIVER-SITY...
...ARE FACING A CRISIS OF GALACTIC PROPOR-TIONS.
SMC
Squid Legs
DOCTOR SHICHCOCK LEADS AN EVIL ORGANI-ZATION KNOWN AS NOUVELLE VAGUE.
THEY ARE BENT ON STEALING THE STUDENTS' MOTIVATION TO STUDY...
...SO THEY CAN RULE THE UNIVER-SITY!
DOCTOR SHICHCOCK'S DAUGHTER IS DISTRESSED BY HER FATHER'S EVIL PLANS, SO SHE SECRETLY DEVELOPS A WARRIOR FOR JUSTICE...
...AND THAT HERO'S NAME IS...

THE SF CLUB AND SMC ARE GOING TO MAKE A MOVIE TOGETHER!!
AND THEY WANT THE ART SQUAD TO HELP!
SMC=SFX Movie Club
The news struck Tomu...
D...
DOES THAT MEAN...
...WE GET TO MAKE A SUPER-HERO MOVIE?!
BBBBB
?!
...like a bolt of lightning!
GRAAAA
Shichikoku University

GORGON...
...FLIP!!!
Wow!!
ISN'T MY NEW MOVE COOL?!
TOMU!! I HAVE BIG NEWS!!

There's the monster!!
It's Gorgonzola!!
THERE THEY ARE! THE SEAFOOD RANGERS!
GASP
One day in early summer...
MWA HA HA HA HA HA HA HA HA
DO YOU THINK YOU CAN STOP ME?!
HERE I COME!!

SCENE 34
Behind the Scenes!!

GLOSSARY

Page 77, panel 6: Takoyaki
Fried octopus balls, a popular festival food.

Page 107, sidebar: 2.5D
These are stage plays and musicals based on manga and anime.

Page 137, panel 2: Taiyaki
Fish-shaped cakes, usually filled with sweet bean paste.

AUTHOR BIO

I started this manga because I wanted to portray the enthusiasm of the people behind the scenes and the growth of a pessimistic individual. I'll be so happy if that got across even a little!

-Bisco Hatori

Bisco Hatori made her manga debut with ***Isshun kan no Romance*** (A Moment of Romance) in ***LaLa DX*** magazine. The comedy ***Ouran High School Host Club*** was her breakout hit and was published in English by VIZ Media. Her other works include ***Detarame Mousouryoku Opera*** (Sloppy Vaporous Opera), ***Petite Pêche!*** and the vampire romance ***Millennium Snow***, which was also published in English by VIZ Media.

Behind the Scenes!!

VOLUME 7

Shojo Beat Edition

STORY AND ART BY **Bisco Hatori**

English Translation & Adaptation/John Werry
Touch-Up Art & Lettering/Sabrina Heep
Design/ J. Shikuma
Editor/Pancha Diaz

Urakata!! by Bisco Hatori

First published in Japan in 2018 by HAKUSENSHA, Inc., Tokyo.
English language translation rights arranged with HAKUSENSHA, Inc., Tokyo.

Printed in the U.S.A.

Published by VIZ Media, LLC
P.O. Box 77010
San Francisco, CA 94107

10 9 8 7 6 5 4 3 2 1
First printing, August 2019

RATED T FOR TEEN

PARENTAL ADVISORY
BEHIND THE SCENES!! is rated T for Teen and is recommended for ages 13 and up.
ratings.viz.com

YOU MAY BE REA
THE WRONG W

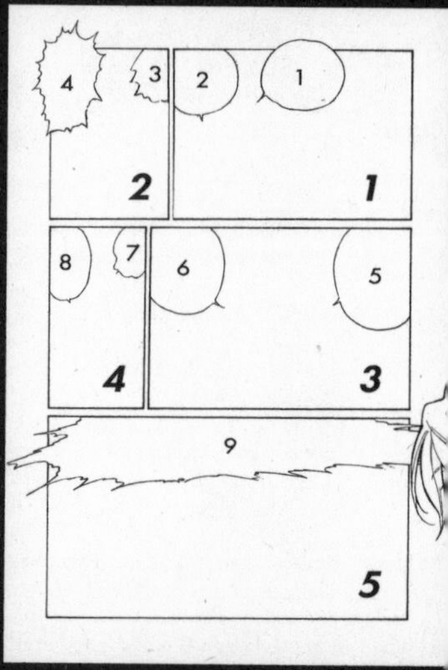

This book reads from right to left to maintain the original presentation and art of the Japanese edition, so action, sound effects and word balloons are reversed. This diagram shows how to follow the panels.
Turn to the other side of the book to begin.